Cooper's New Challenge

Author and Photographer
Susan Brown-Wadleigh

All rights reserved. No part of this publication may be reproduced or transmitted in any form, or by any means electronic or mechanical including, photocopying, recording, or by any retrieval system without prior written permission from the author.

Copyright © 2023 Susan Brown-Wadleigh

All rights reserved.

ISBN: 979-8-218-26107-8

DEDICATION

To my family whose continuing support is why I keep doing what I do. To the students at Twitchell Elementary School who encourage me to keep writing. To the pets of the world who teach us that love is unconditional.

CONTENTS

	Acknowledgments	5
1	Cooper's New Challenge	Pg 6
2	Rocket's Story	Pg 9
3	Rocket Gets a New Name	Pg 12
4	Snugs Gets a Condo	Pg 20
5	Cooper Teaches Snugs How to Pose	Pg 23
6	Friends	Pg 26

ACKNOWLEDGMENTS

When I decided a rabbit would be a good addition to my new household, I looked up rescues in my area and found Bunnies Matter. My son and I drove out to their adoption center on a Saturday in April, just to look. The bunnies were housed in an old, converted milking barn There were several rows of roomy enclosures. Most of them had two bunnies residing. I recognized some of the rabbits from the pictures online. On the second level of the barn was a little orange bunny alone in his enclosure. He was looking for a way out. He hopped to us, checked me over, then kept on exploring his new space. "This is the rabbit," I thought. He was curious, calm, and fearless. Just what I wanted as a friend for my blind dog. As I started the adoption process it was clear that the organization was setting me up for success. For the low fee they were asking they provided all the supplies that were needed from the enclosure to bags of hay, and litter tray. All rabbits were neutered or spayed and had necessary injections. I went home with a very in-depth packet of care information.

There are many rabbit rescue organizations in Nevada working hard to find homes for abandoned bunnies. They all campaign hard for spay and neuter legislation. For more information about Bunnies Matter please contact www.bunniesmatter.org.

Thank you to Bunnies Matter for the use of three of their pictures on page 9 and page 11. They are the adoption sign, the bunnies in the field and the adoption center.

Chapter 1   Cooper's New Challenge

Cooper the cocker spaniel's life had been turned upside down. First, his beloved dad passed away. Then he and his mom moved into a new home. Cooper was sad and confused.

One day, while resting quietly in his new home, Cooper felt something sniffing at his nose. The curious dog's ears perked up and he began to sniff back.

Mom said, "This is Rocket. He is going to join us on our new adventure."

As soon as their noses touched Rocket sensed that Cooper was different.

Rocket's new brother was blind.

Chapter 2   Rocket's Story

Rocket was a "dumped" bunny.

This means that his family no longer wanted to care for him so they "dumped" him at a park alone and in danger.

Luckily for our little rabbit there was a kind security guard who knew what to do.

He scooped up the bunny and took him to a caring volunteer at a nearby rabbit shelter.

Adoption day was a whirlwind. The little rabbit barely had time to explore his pen when a happy voice said, "This is the one. This is my bunny!"

Chapter 3   Rocket Gets a New Name

Rocket started to explore his new home right away!

He looked in things.

He looked on things.

He even discovered the joy of watching old movies!

Everywhere Rocket went Cooper followed.

They ate lettuce and carrots together. Cooper ate most of it.

When Cooper accidentally walked over Rocket, the rabbit never got mad.

One day when Cooper was napping, Rocket hopped on the bed next to the sleeping dog.

The brave bunny inched closer...

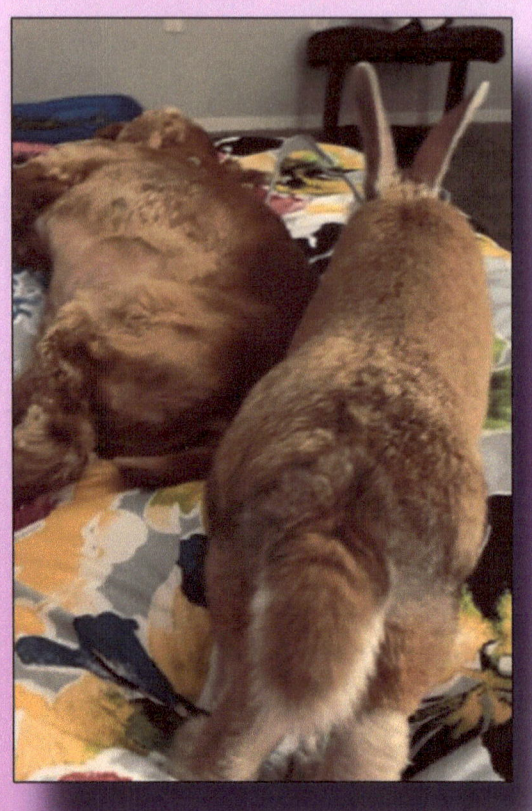

and closer...

and closer.

Until he couldn't **GET** any closer!

"You are not a Rocket," said mom. "You are a snuggle bunny. From now on we will call you Snugs!"

Chapter 4   Snugs Gets a Condo

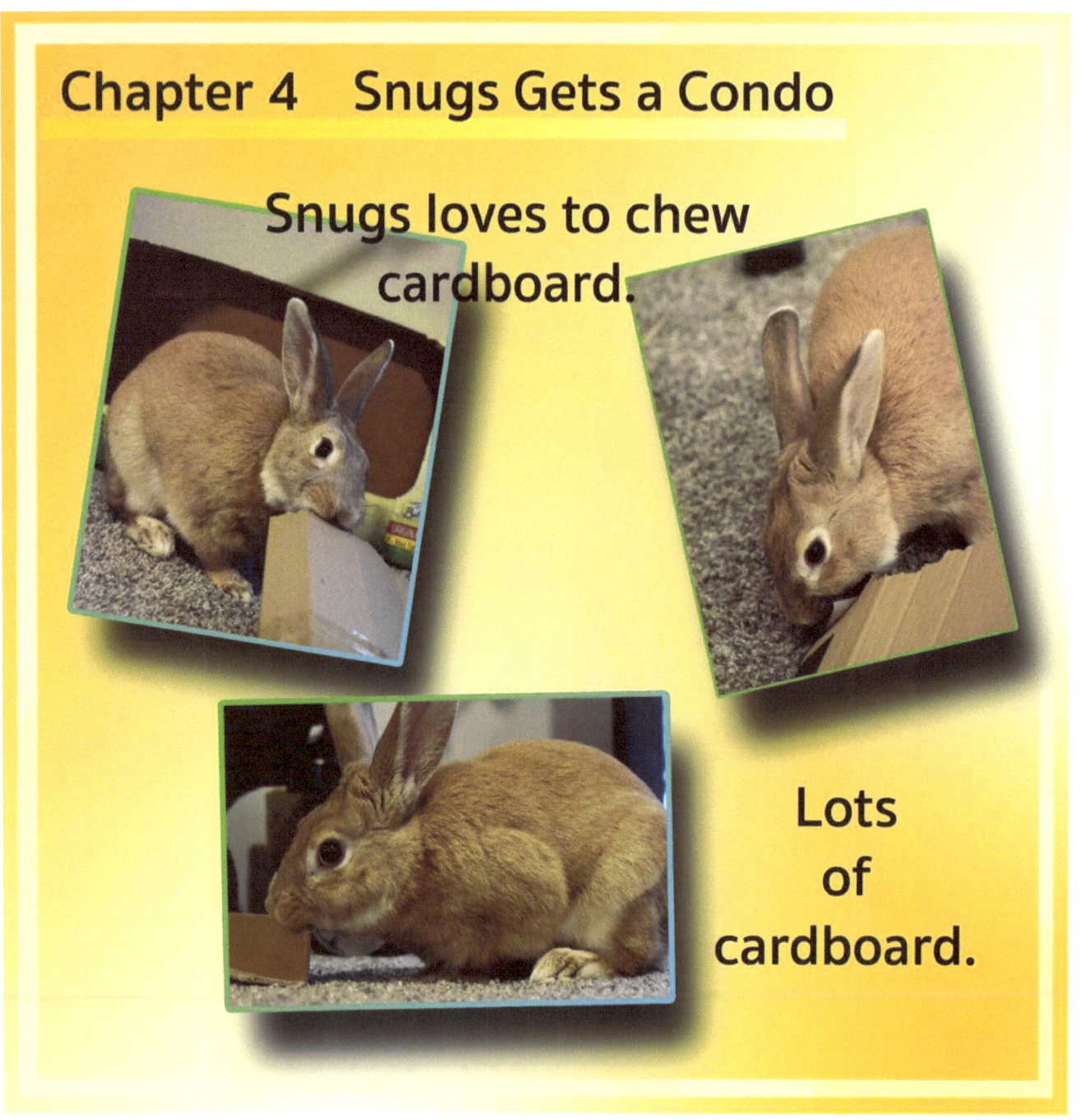

Snugs loves to chew cardboard.

Lots of cardboard.

Snugs jumped for joy when a huge box arrived. Better than the cardboard was the house inside.

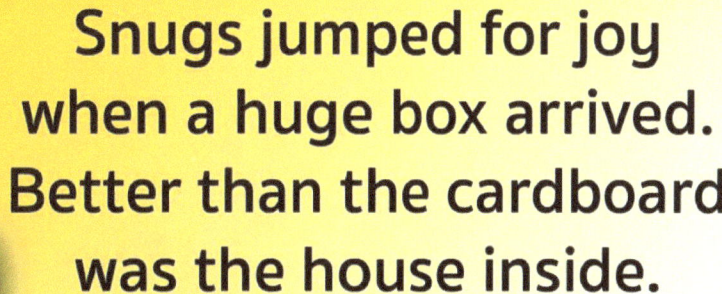

Cooper and Snugs supervised the building of the new house.

They checked every floor...

and every door.

Snugs' House

He showed his friend,
Smoke the guinea pig
the trick to posing:
demand a lot of lettuce!

Chapter 6   Friends

Snugs is never far away from Cooper.

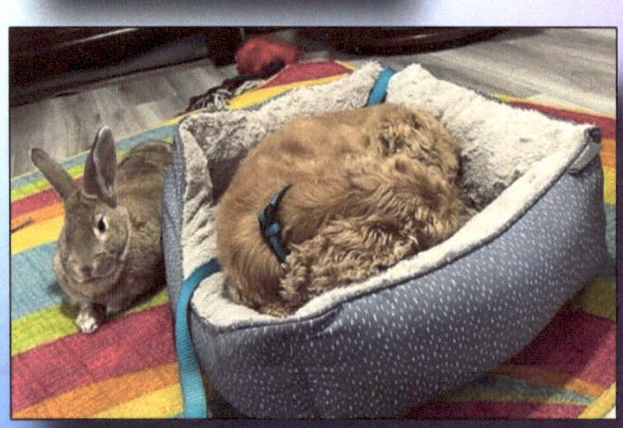

They share fun, food, and family.

Cooper's and Snugs' friendship began with loss.

Now their friendship is based on kindness and love.

Cooper

Snugs

ABOUT THE AUTHOR

Susan Brown-Wadleigh lives with her cocker spaniel Cooper, and her fearless rabbit Snugs. She is the proud parent to son Ben.

Other Books Available by

Susan Brown-Wadleigh

on Amazon.com

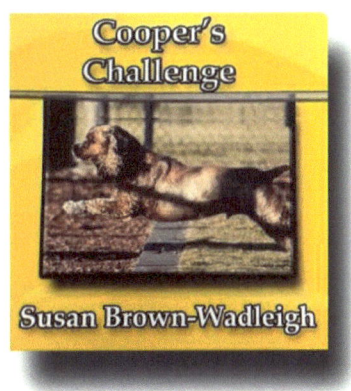

www.ingramcontent.com/pod-product-compliance
Lightning Source LLC
Chambersburg PA
CBHW041538040426
42446CB00002B/139